Old Men
in JEANS

Cover picture by the author
Cover design: Y Lolfa

ISBN: 987 - 1 - 84771 - 434 - 3

Published and printed in Wales on paper from
sustainable forests by Y Lolfa Cyf., Talybont,
Ceredigion SY24 5HE
website www.ylolfa.com
e-mail ylolfa@ylolfa.com
tel. 01970 832 304
fax 01970 832 782

Old Men *in* JEANS

Peter Walker

y Lolfa

people…

Old Men in Jeans

"Ah-hah!" the young ones cry
pointing supercilious fingers
"Who do they think they are?"
belt cinched tight
beneath the paunch
grey-if-any hair
an amble and a stroll
but
once
we were the first
unafraid
to sport our tans
below the navel and above the knee
thrust our thighs like thunder…
look hard
you fashion Pharisees
what we are you will one day be
but
what we were…
ah…
what we were!

The Dive

she arched her back
in feline somnolence
to wake each hillocked follicle
& posed
Minerva-like
toes fingering the chiselled edge
of the flexed board

& then the gentle parabola of grace
the momentum of exhilaration
the barely heard applause of blue

she laughs the water from her eyes
as she rises
dripping freedom from every pore

Organising Louise

you see, it's very easy...
here in the drawer marked 'work' you keep work:
>   shocking cinema
>   feminism
>   French new wave
here on these CDs you have:
>   New York & other holidays
>   Rachel's piss-up, friends & party pics
>   assorted family including cat
& in these drawers should be:
>   neat rows of sorted underwear and matching socks
>   T-shirts here and blouses there
>   gym-kit, jumpers, miscellaneous tops

we do this
to keep the chaos out
fearing
lest the
less we organise
the more the meaningless creeps in
seeking solace
in a structure we can understand

but
she is not here
she is working out
her own route
through this messy bedroom world

S.

the warmth beside me
warms
the coldness in my bones
the shape beside me
fits my shape
a jigsaw of souls
our breaths are corollary
in to my out
out to my in
the charcoal line between us
blurred & feint
leaving just a pencil scratch
to mark
the difference of our skins

I woke with the rain

I woke with the rain
louder by far than
the soft tide of your breath
& as the finger circled
past the sickle-hour
so roof & gutter
rippled with a show of joy

& later
the silent beauty of the stars
in the half-light
roused you

their brittle pulse
would not be washed away

The Tree Man

once I cut down trees

lopped heavy boughs
mossy & arthritic
so bent the heavy apples
rested their green plumpness
on the September grass

sawed through the holly trunk
releasing thorns & nails
& swept them up
to spare the toddlers' tears

took the axe
to storm-downed ash or elm
& watched the chips of white flesh drip
until the logs were stacked
ready for the drying and the fire

my limbs were strong
my back stronger
to bear the burden
of wood & others' worry

but now
my boughs are bent
& my skin pales
without the yellow sun to lick it

the axe & saw
are in another's hands
& he is waiting at the gate

Twenty-two
(in memory of my father)

in this photograph
my age at graduation
a graduate of a different world

thin lips attempt a smile
weighed down by TNT & browning shell
face white as searchlight beam
eyes pricked by tears
& dancing glow of bonfires
far below
tracer trail on retina
flesh ripped thin
by corkscrew dive
& lurch of fear in stomach pit
& thirty times & more this test was sat
& passed
while others failed the stern questioning
& were sent down
to die
in flame or field or sea

there is relief
the shoulders droop
but in survival
the price of certainty is paid
if all is random, chance...
what point belief?

there is only now…
the bettering, day by day
for
eternity is lapped up by dogs
in blast-blown ruined streets

we did not talk of this
but
each knew that the other knew

The Greenhouse

the old priest grew tomatoes
he pushed the seeds into the warm soil
& offered them the bounty of God's mercy
day by sun-bleached day
pouring fresh life
from the cracked & pitted aluminium
of his soul

he pricked out the seedlings
making room for them to grow & flourish
& repotted them carefully
his once deft fingers
grimed with compost
collecting dirt beneath brittle, yellowing nails

as the plants
stretched veiny leaves to face the light
so his veiny hands
tended the gentle, yellow flowers
to bud
& bring them to sumptuousness of flesh
red & moist

& all the long days of summer
you could find him within his glass sanctuary
comforting the lost
crying with the grieving
holding the bereft

as tenderly as he would the rootlets
which he teased
to plump fullness of life
with his caring hands

Michelangelo paints the Madonna
(Florence, 1528)

Where is she
this model for a pretty pose?

I searched long among the
corpses at Benedetto's
but
their sword-pierced, sad
drowned, consumptive or world-lost faces
wore too much the
bloom of death

but then I saw her

holding her bundle tight against her breast
a child protected by a child
a sister's strange, protective love
swathed against the shards of rain
head covered
eyes lowered
humble lest she catch the gaze
of one above her station

how cruel the world
to learn so much so young!
a curriculum of misery
complete at thirteen years

"Will you sit for me?"
"Sit? Yes! A coin will buy you more!"
"Just… sit. Strike a pose. Stare at the light.
Imagine angels with good news."
"Good news? Good news? God knows what that might be!"
"Put down the child."

"Put down the child! Sir, he is my son!"

The Jesus Tattoo

Michael is a modern monk
enclosed within the monastery of his disability
the vow of silence
taken by his brain one summer
when bird-song sang above his wordless cry
so now he speaks
with the vocabulary of his inked sleeve
from shoulder blade to wrist
words that thread through petals
& interweave within the knotwork
he points to his own quiet mystery & the path he walks

in the day-room
the lingering smell of illicit cigarettes
the smoke still heavy as the valley mist

& Michael bares his bicep
to show the Titian head with its crown of thorns
& as he flexes his muscle
so the face will fill with
pain & compassion in equal measure
& Michael joins his salty tears to the pale-blue painted drops
& in this coalescence he becomes a sacred heart
teaching me the meaning of salvation

... place...

Eglwys St Grwst

disenfranchised by language:

lost in an alien sea of words
I am adrift
in crashing waves of vocabulary
in swell of mutations
in tidal pull of ancient bardic vowels
that write verses in my soul
& yet I cannot catch the rhyme

& this we do
week by week:
the selfsame comfortable words
in a voice we know
our innate fluency untranslated
in a foreign ear

better by far to learn another tongue
to set the heart on fire

fight alienation with community
& hopelessness with faith

speak words of life & love & hope
of freedom, caring, trust
compassion, healing, peace
new life…

On Pydew Hill

on Pydew hill
the bell rang out Ascensiontide

cotton-white dawn
pressed & linen-fresh
tight-tucked
beneath a jaundiced cataract of sun
wraith-like rises
wisp from purple thistle-head
from dappled dog-rose
losing eyes of dew

& then the word...

from button valley
to the sweep of blue
from Maelgwn's stones
to embrace of love
from tower & keep
to giving heart

& Pentecost is soon

Hive (Seiriol's Cell)

circlet of stones
carried a-stumble from shore & cliff
dug from pliant dust
map out the circumference

god-factory
once thrumming with the buzz of prayer
one-man band of holy tunes
huddled beneath daub & wattle
with the tide beat
borne
now loud now soft
upon the ural air

the bees may fly again…
& from these desert bards
there drips the honey
of the three-leaf clover bud

The Trees of Noddfa

pines stretch high
through soup of mist
to catch the first warmth
a halo of black crows
dances round the tip-top point
feathers sleek with sun-drop

the yew spreads wide
to shelter mouse & pecking sparrow
& guard them from the droplet grey
& keep the arrow-north breeze
at bough's length

pine & yew together
hold up passion's banner
& become the cross
which teaches us
the inner truth of faith

St Trillo's Chapel

broken-backed coracle of a place
beneath the hump-back road
by the storm-bent trees
small enough for
half the weary congregations
in these last-gasp days
lingering piss-smell for incense
choir of craking gulls
& organ drone of wave
while there
the lost hint of fellowship
for all the worn-out pilgrims
locked behind a prison grille
weighed down with altar stone
unchain me, it says
let the oppressed go free
release me from these dark dungeons
& let me run into the aching blue
just as I did before

Llangystennin

squat box of care-chiselled stone
footings gentle in soft soil
as much a part of this created earth
as the arms of ivy that
embracing
hold it anchored in spinning space
the single bell
calling from the west
its arthritic, rusty joints
ache & groan at pull of rope
frayed by constancy of
crusted hand & glove of lace
draws us east
where hounds run free
where
prised from dogma chains & nails
we wear the tonsure of our history
& drink the wine of freedom
tabernacled in love

The Company of Saints

I preside
at the table of ghosts
before me
in the shadows
the scattered few
are hemmed in by
a cloud of silent witnesses
who rattle windows
& turn the pages with a sigh

the polished oak
is peopled with fractal colours
mocking ordinary time

there is a sparseness to our phrasing
& echoing in the hollowness between
come angel voices –
he is not here…

Two Liverpool Poems

(i)   Liverpool 1
(written during the work on rebuilding Liverpool 1)

hard-faced long-nosed girls
with trowels of orange make-up
cracks plastered
a half-built city of a face
          like
Church Street

*   *   *

there are cranes over Paradise

*   *   *

crop-headed lads
displaying labels
inside-out lives
          like
insects
structure shielding
soft mellow mallow
gloss hiding hints
of deep dock water
– but how to swim?

girls with hair dyed

red as an Anfield shirt
bleached beach blonde
ash streaks
curled like a Davy Crocket hat
– eyes drawn upwards

tabard tops over jeans
onion layers
"I am in here
          but
I will not be seen
or touched"

*   *   *

somewhere
there is a heart
surrounded by boards
and 'no entry' signs
beneath the concrete rouge
behind the staccato accent
of the drill
swathed in Gap glass
and Oasis steel
"If I am loved
          then
I am weak
– aren't I?"

*   *   *

lift the nave
make room
for
rebuilding broken lives

*   *   *

there are cranes over Paradise

(ii)   Big Bill Broonzy meets Vivienne Westwood
(a poem for two voices)

there are flowers for Billy Fury
at Pier Head
a tear for each of a thousand eyes

meanwhile…

Big Bill Broonzy
is on
Mathew Street

the times they sure are a-changin'
yet the dreams they stay the same

fire-brick eyes stare coldly
across the cobbles
at the neon signature

pre-rock prince
                            post-punk princess
stretched tonic suit
                            bondage trousers
flicking sweat off pomaded hair
                            where the shop once called 'Sex'?
loud and dirty
                            catwalk prissy
paid in tumblers of scotch
                            paid in gold-card candy
anarchy in the bones
                            anarchy as an idea
freedom marches
                            freedom lounges
revolution in my heart
                            revolution on my T-shirt
blues in my soul
                            blue might be the next black
heavy measures
                            light as a feather

Big Bill Broonzy
Big Joe Turner
Big Bobby Blue Bland

blow your harps in paradise and set the angels bopping
swing that axe for Billy
and make these streets alive
again…
… again

Here

here
heavy with possibility
history scribed across the landscape
with its saints & archaeology
its mines & quarries
& their squat, dark men
whose shadows fall still
across beach & valley

the lilt of osprey wings
that dive for food
in glacier melt
clockwork toy of oyster-catchers
sprinting in relays
along the damp, wet sand of Traeth Lafan
dipping beaks to touch lost lands

& in this mix of
people, place & other signs of grace
we hold the mirror to still lips
& find
the misty morning breath
that signals life –
deep, deep stirrings
as high as Tryfan &
as deep as any soul

… & other signs of grace…

After Baudelaire
(Correspondances)

Look: nature is a tower of living stone
Which lets a Babel babble flow, and we
All-knowing, fail to hear the forest moan,
But yet it watches us who stay or flee.
Like echoes long which merge and interplay,
Each perfume, colour, taste or smell or sound,
All hint at correspondance, vast as day,
As deep as midnight darkness (blue … profound).
There are yet scents as fresh and cool as flesh,
As soft as oboes (plaintive, green as field),
While others (rich, perverse) entrap, enmesh
Or free the soul – infinity revealed!
Thus incense, musk and sandalwood combined
Release ecstatic senses… free the mind!

Thaw
(late December)

the uncleared autumn leaves
surprise at snow-melt
curled & black & still as spider corpse
with velvet sheen of hoar-moss

the ghost-grey hump of dirty path-clear
pocked with grit & gravel
edge as crisp as fried egg-white at dawn
leaks life
until we lose all memory
save the mind's eye snap
of bride-white upon the Carnedd
&
we dream again
of all that cruel purity
&
virgin birth

Jesus Jazz

I practise hard
working the familiar chords
until they are part of me
& I strum out the rhythm
drawing back
the wild screech-note saxophone
the be-pretty-bop clarinet
curdled trumpet
reminding them in their inner ear
of the constant theme
around which they improvise
to make music
for these troubled times

Coracle

so we make shapes
with the crude instrument of our imaginings
snail-shell spiral
circumference of sun
arc of crescent moon
diameter of horizon
we take the willow
six months in the drying
& weave the basket of our dreamscape
such prosaic preparation
stitched with sinuous care
plump with promise
becomes
the hollow apricot of hope

Ash Wednesday

we pronounce the words
of our own demise
this last generation
of the orthodox

like the grey dust
warm, bereft
raked from the cremator
we are piled high
& scattered
by the agnostic wind
specks of carbon falling
star-dross on a different earth

but from this passing
we wait
on Holy Saturday
for the spice of resurrection

it may yet come...
seedling prayer in house & home
begins to sprout a different shoot
& if it comes to bloom
outside these treasured walls
we should applaud its prescience
& give it room to grow

Young Gulls

as Michaelmas sweats its way through harvest
& mouths a final yawn of summer
before the leaves curl & drop
like dried & brittle spider shells
beneath the window sills
so the young gulls
fallow-dappled
big as ravens
hungry & persistent
strut their way between Gloddaeth Crescent & the sea
between the easy bounty of the promenade
& the harsher need to fend & dive
unsure
if they really want to moult to ash & white
for they are quite at home
in between
in their ruffled rags
calling
calling for one last craw
that does not come

The Wild Geese

steely musculature of evolution
ball & socket greased within
could thrust my weight aside with one slow beat
wild eye that will refuse the taming

& now
the antique calling has begun again
senses attuned to this new time
a hint of earth birth in nasal bone
of wood & iron
of knot in stone
the salty seaweed now evolves fresh dreams
there is an ache that kneads
this seeming impossibility of flight
to mystic fruition

& now
pencil grey against the clouds
the flick & glide & steady pull
beneath the rising swell of cumulus
the ancient calls that rise in throats in flight
inviting those who gaze in fear & awe
to flex their fledgling feathers
& begin eternity
in the grace of air

Rooks

rooks are barking
like seals
in the sycamore trees
swimming in the blue tide of sky
& beaching on the green shore of branches
then launching off the spur of bough
while
one disdainful gull
flaunting its stately grace
tacks across infinity
& looks aghast at rook & sparrow
tumbling in the currents close to shore

Stars

swirling cacophonous tribe of gulls
announcing
the deepening redness in the west
& as the purple bruise
swells
& fills the void of sky
so their voices
one by one
fall silent in wonder
at the mystery of stars

The Morning Office

whatever time or season
the silted oil
slow to wake
gurgles its slow course around
sclerotic pipes

baking beach-filled August
or
numbing winter frost
here
a little west of heaven
it is always ten degrees below

blown in like scattered grain
we gather
black-plumed brood
shepherded beneath those wider wings
to hear again the stories of our soul
& turn the grimy pages
made transparent by our turning

renewed
we seek to be the broken crumbs
that drop the seeds of life
into the cracks beneath our feet